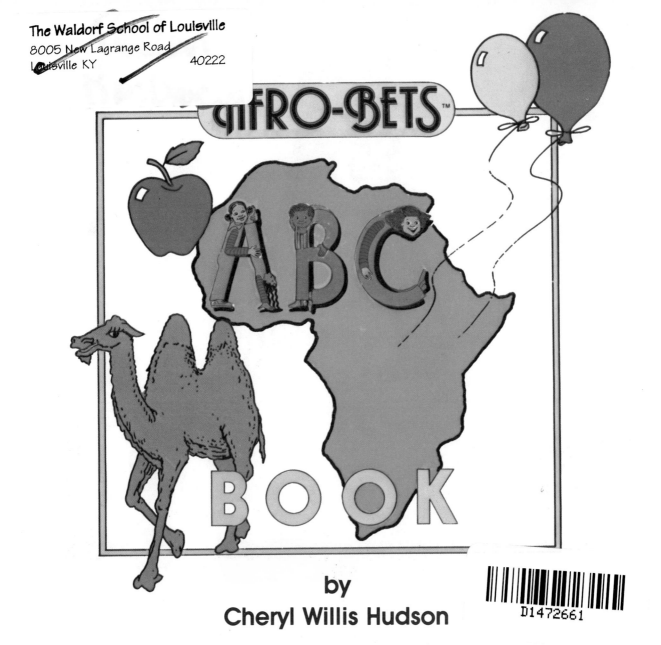

by

Cheryl Willis Hudson

AFRO-BETS™ is a trademark of Cheryl Willis Hudson. The AFRO-BETS™ Kids were conceived and created by Wade Hudson and Cheryl Willis Hudson. Pictures are rendered by Culverson Blair after original illustrations by the author. Inquiries should be addressed to JUST US BOOKS, a division of Just Us Productions, Inc., 301 Main Street, Orange, NJ 07050.
Printed in the United States of America   First Edition   Library of Congress Catalog Card Number 87-81580   ISBN: 0-940975-00-9.

apple

A a  Africa

alligator

baseball

B

B b   balloons

baby

car

C c

camel

cornrows

doll

D d

dog

dancers

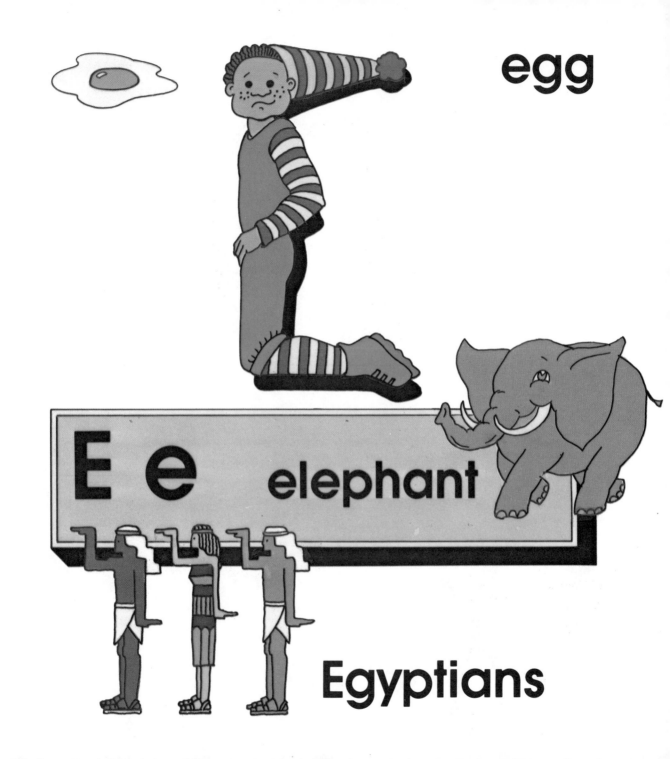

egg

E e   elephant

Egyptians

football

F f   feather

fish

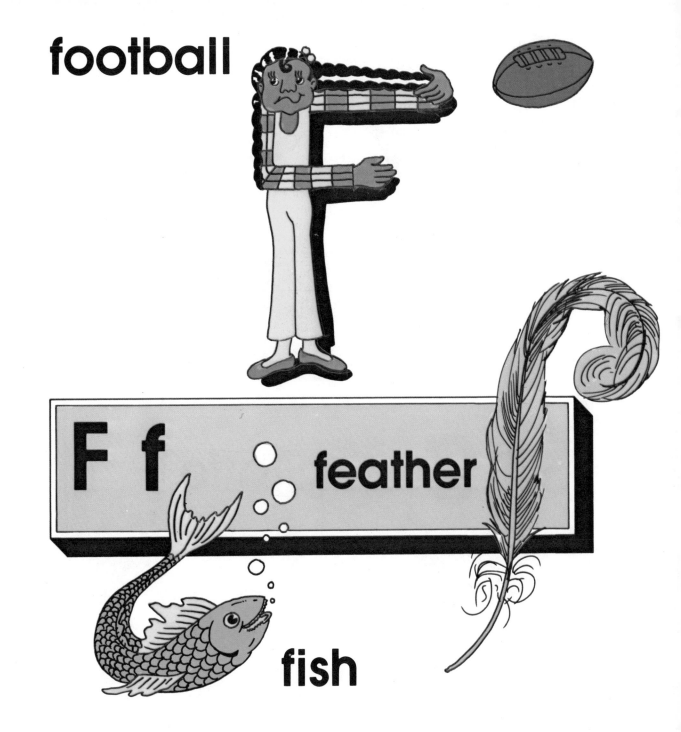

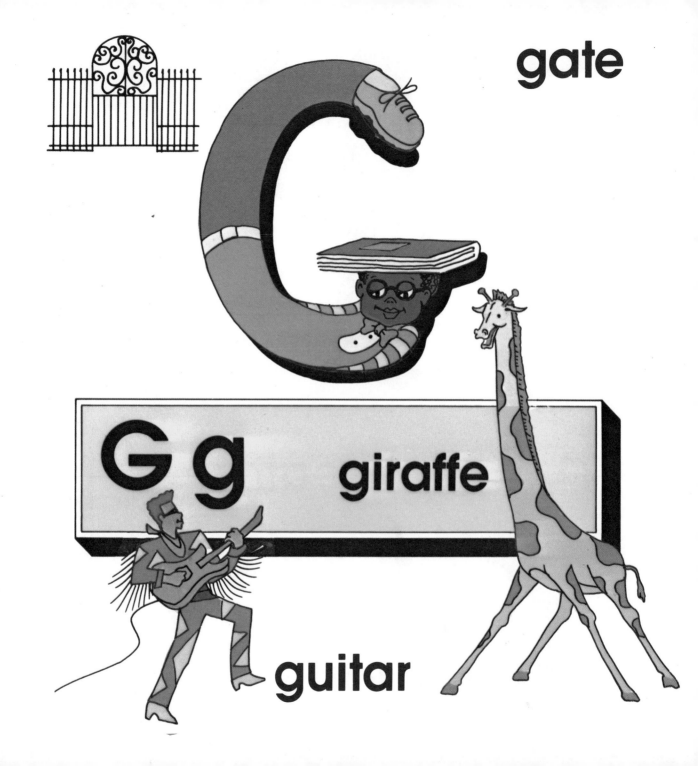

gate

G g giraffe

guitar

hotdog

H h house

hippo

ivory

I i

ice cream

iron

jet

J j jumprope

jaguar

kitten

K k   keys

Kente cloth

lips

L l

lion

ladybug

mask

Mm monkey

magician

nose

N

Nn   Nefertiti

9
nine

orange

onion

octopus

O o

peanuts

P p

pencil

panda

queen

Q q quilt

question mark

rose

R

rainbow

rhinoceros

stop

S s sun

sphinx

television

T t   tulip

turtle

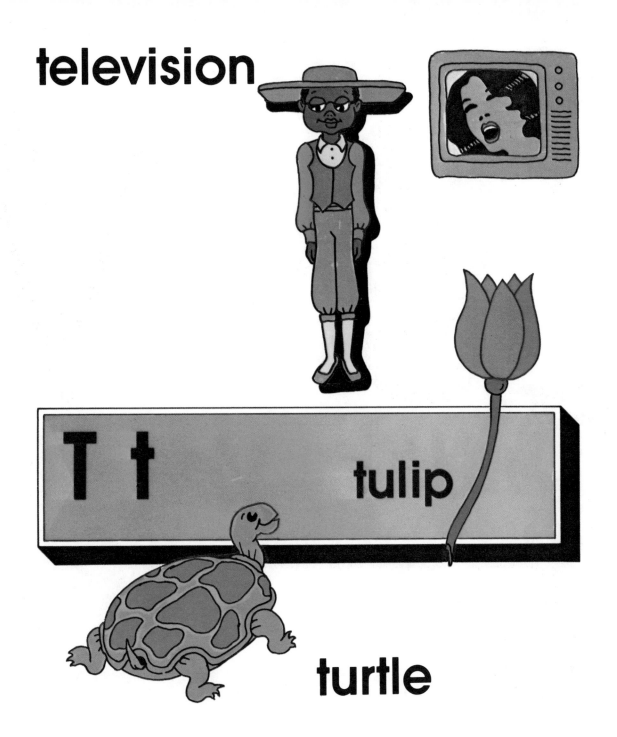

umbrella

valentine

U u V v

unicycle   volcano

window xylophone

W w X x

wagon X-ray

yam

zipper

Yy

Zz

yarn

zebra